The Israelites had disobeyed God. They would not listen to him any more. Very soon the Midianites, who lived close to them, began to raid their land. They stole food and animals from the Israelites.

The Israelites were hungry and frightened. They hid in caves in the hills. And they cried out to God to help them.

One of the Israelites was called Gideon.
When he was still a little boy, he had
heard wonderful stories about God from
his father and grandfather.

Gideon heard how Moses and the
Israelites had escaped from Egypt with
God's help.

Gideon
fights for God

Story by Penny Frank

Illustrated by Tony Morris

THE LION
STORY BIBLE

13

OXFORD · BATAVIA · SYDNEY

The Bible tells us how God chose the Israelites to be his special people. He made them a promise that he would always love and care for them. But they must obey him.

God rescued them from Egypt and led them into the promised land. With Joshua as their leader they trusted God and drove out their enemies. But before long they disobeyed God and were in trouble again.

This is the story of how God sent Gideon to set them free from one of their enemies.

You can find the story in your own Bible, in Judges, chapters 6 and 7.

Copyright © 1987 Lion Publishing

Published by
Lion Publishing plc
Sandy Lane West, Oxford, England
ISBN 0 85648 738 4
ISBN 0 7459 1758 5 (paperback)
Lion Publishing Corporation
1705 Hubbard Avenue, Batavia, Illinois 60510, USA
ISBN 0 85648 738 4
Albatross Books Pty Ltd
PO Box 320, Sutherland, NSW 2232, Australia
ISBN 0 86760 522 7
ISBN 0 7324 0078 8 (paperback)

First edition 1987, reprinted 1988, 1990
Paperback edition 1989

British Library Cataloguing in
Publication Data

Frank, Penny
  Gideon fights of God. – (The Lion
  Story Bible; 13)
  1. Gideon – Juvenile literature
  I. Title   II. Morris, Tony, 1938 Aug 2 –
  222'.320924   BS580.G5

ISBN 0-85648-738-4
ISBN 0-7459-1758-5 (paperback)

Printed in Yugoslavia

Library of Congress Cataloging in
Publication Data

Frank, Penny.
Gideon fights for God.
(The Lion Story Bible; 13)
1. Gideon (Biblical judge) – Juvenile
literature. 2. Bible. O.T. – Biography –
Juvenile literature. 3. Bible stories,
English – O.T. Judges. [1. Gideon (Biblical
judge) 2. Bible stories – O.T.]
I. Morris, Tony, ill. II. Title. III. Series:
Frank, Penny. Lion Story Bible; 13.
BS580.G5F73 1987   222'.3209505
86-18523
ISBN 0-85648-738-4
ISBN 0-7459-1758-5 (paperback)

'Where is God now?' Gideon asked. 'We need him to fight against these Midianites.'

Gideon did not know that God had a special plan for him when he was grown-up.

When Gideon was a young man, an angel of God came to visit him. Gideon was not sure who it was.

'God wants you to lead his people to fight the Midianites,' the angel said. 'There is no need to be afraid. God will be with you.'

But Gideon was frightened.

'I can't do that,' he said. 'I'm not important enough.'

'You can do it, because God will help you,' said the angel.

Then the angel went away.

But Gideon could not believe that God had spoken to him.

So he asked God for proof.

'If you really want me to fight the Midianites,' he said to God, 'please give me a sign.'

So that night, Gideon put a sheepskin outside the cave. In the morning it was wet with dew but the ground all around was dry!

But Gideon still could not believe that God had spoken to him.

'I need to be really sure,' he said to God. So he put out the sheepskin again. 'Please don't be angry. Will you do it again, the other way around?'

Next morning, the sheepskin was dry but the ground all around was wet with dew! Now Gideon was really sure.

Gideon called the Israelites out of hiding
and got them ready for battle. There
were thousands of men in the army.

When they were ready, God said, 'You
have too many men. I want you to be
sure that I have won the battle, not you.'

So Gideon told the men, 'Anyone who is afraid can go home.'

Many of the men were frightened, and so more than half the army went back home.

God said, 'Now Gideon, you still have too many men. Watch them drinking at the river. Most of them are drinking with their faces right down to the water. They are not looking out for the enemy. Send them home.

'The men who are scooping the water up to their mouths with their hands are ready for anything to happen,' said God. 'With that small group of men I will win the battle against the Midianites.' Now there were only three hundred men left.

'I promise that I will be with you,' God said to Gideon. 'But if you are afraid, go down and listen outside the Midianites' tents.'

So Gideon crept down to where the Midianites were camping. He heard them say, 'Gideon is going to win. God has given him victory.'

Then Gideon knew that even their enemies believed God would win the battle.

As soon as it was dark, Gideon sent his army off in three groups.

Each man carried a large jar, a flaming torch and a trumpet.

'Keep the torch hidden inside the jar,' said Gideon. 'Don't make a sound until I give the signal. Then copy everything I do.'

19

The three groups of men crept down to the tents of the Midianites.

When Gideon was ready, he smashed his jar, blew his trumpet and shouted, 'A sword for the Lord and for Gideon!'

All around the camp his men did the same.

The torches flamed in a great circle. The Midianites woke up to hear the blast of trumpets and the shouting. It sounded like a great army.

In the dark they could not see who they were fighting. They even fought their own men by mistake. Then they all ran away.

21

The Israelites danced and celebrated their victory. They were so glad that Gideon had been brave enough to obey God and be their leader.

'We really are sorry we were so disobedient before,' they told God. 'Now we want to be your people in the land you have given us.'

The Lion Story Bible is made up of 52 individual stories for young readers, building up an understanding of the Bible as one story — God's story — a story for all time and all people.

The Old Testament section (numbers 1–30) tells the story of a great nation — God's chosen people, the Israelites — and God's love and care for them through good times and bad. The stories are about people who knew and trusted God. From this nation came one special person, Jesus Christ, sent by God to save all people everywhere.

The story of Gideon comes from the Old Testament book of Judges, chapters 6–8. The battle is in chapter 7.
   Although the Israelites took possession of the land of Canaan, they did not finish the job of driving out their enemies. Before long they found themselves under attack from all sides. They had deserted God and begun to worship the gods of the peoples around them. But when things got really bad, they cried to God for help — and he sent them champions, one after the other, to help them drive out their enemies.
   Gideon was one of God's champions. He took his orders from God. And it was God who won the battle for his people. So they learned the lesson of obedience, for a little while.
   The next book in this series is number 14: *Samson, the strong man*. It tells the astonishing story of another of God's champions.